Light in the Real World

by Robin Koontz

Content Consultant
Justin Peatross
Professor of Physics
Brigham Young University

CORE
LIBRARY

Published by ABDO Publishing Company, PO Box 398166, Minneapolis, MN 55439. Copyright © 2013 by Abdo Consulting Group, Inc. International copyrights reserved in all countries. No part of this book may be reproduced in any form without written permission from the publisher. The Core Library™ is a trademark and logo of ABDO Publishing Company.

Printed in the United States of America,
North Mankato, Minnesota
112012
012013
♻ THIS BOOK CONTAINS AT LEAST 10% RECYCLED MATERIALS.

Editor: Karen Latchana Kenney
Series Designer: Becky Daum

Cataloging-in-Publication Data
Koontz, Robin.
 Light in the real world / Robin Koontz.
   p. cm. -- (Science in the real world)
Includes bibliographical references and index.
ISBN 978-1-61783-791-3
1. Light--Juvenile literature.   I. Title.
535--dc21

                                            2012946820

Photo Credits: Shutterstock Images, cover, 1, 21, 29, 39, 41; Jo Ann Snover/Shutterstock Images, 4; NASA, 7; Red Line Editorial, 8, 20; Pete Niesen/Shutterstock Images, 9; DK Images, 10; Imagno/Getty Images, 13; Christopher Powers/Bloomberg/Getty Images, 15; Willyam Bradberry/Shutterstock Images, 18, 45; Jane McIlroy/Shutterstock Images, 23; S J Francis/Shutterstock Images, 26; Yuri Arcurs/Shutterstock Images, 31; Olga Miltsova/Shutterstock Images, 32; Jamie Cooper/SSPL/Getty Images, 34; Tim Graham/Getty Images, 36

CONTENTS

CHAPTER ONE

The Light in Your Life

At night you flip on a light switch, and your bedroom lights up. In the morning the sun shines brightly through your bedroom window. Outside plants and trees flourish in the sunshine. Without the sun's light, plants and trees would not be able to grow. Most of life on Earth depends on light to see and survive. Plants and trees would die without light. What would happen if the sun disappeared?

The sun shines through a window, lighting up the room inside.

Food from Light

Plants can produce their own food with just light, air, and water. This amazing process is called photosynthesis. Chlorophyll in plants combines the sun's energy and carbon dioxide to create a sugar. The plant uses some of the sugar for energy and growth and stores the rest.

People might survive for a while. But life as we know it would perish without the sun. So just what is light?

Visible Light

The light that we see with our eyes is called visible light. It is made of energy. Visible light is part of the electromagnetic (EM) spectrum. We see this light in many different colors. The EM spectrum also includes energy that we cannot see.

Our eyes are really just light detectors. The retina at the back of the eye responds to visible light. We can't see anything at all in total darkness.

It is dark at night because we are on the shaded side of Earth. At night the sun is still shining, but Earth has rotated. It is daytime on parts of Earth that face

A view of Earth from space shows half of the planet lit by the sun with the other half in total darkness.

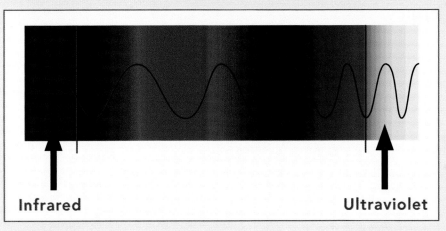

Infrared   **Ultraviolet**

The Electromagnetic Spectrum

We see light waves as the colors of the rainbow. All of the waves together create white light. This diagram shows the different kinds of light on the EM spectrum. Take a look at this diagram. Compare how the information is conveyed visually in the diagram with how it's conveyed in the text. How are the diagram and text similar? How are the diagram and text different?

the sun. Earth spins completely around during a 24-hour period. This creates night and day throughout the world.

Light All Around Us

The sun is the main source of light on Earth. The bright moon does not make its own light. It reflects light from the sun. But there are other kinds of light. Lightning is an electric current in the clouds. Stars light up the night sky. They are very hot balls of gas

A box jellyfish creates a kind of light in its body.

like the sun. The sun happens to be the closest star to Earth. That's why it is the brightest. Heat from a fire also can create light. Even some plants and animals glow in the dark.

Scientists have studied the nature of light for hundreds of years. They are still discovering new things about the mystery of light.

CHAPTER TWO

Bright Ideas

Light means life. The sun has been lighting and warming Earth for more than 4 billion years. More than 400,000 years ago people started using fire, another important source of light and warmth. People built fires to cook their food. The fire kept them warm and helped keep animals away. People created simple lamps made of plant fiber and grease in shells or stone bowls. Oil lamps were built

Ancient humans used fire for light, warmth, protection, and cooking food.

from animal horns or clay pottery. People could light their homes and travel in the dark with these lamps.

By 8000 BCE people had also discovered how to make good use of the sun's energy for food. They grew and harvested plants. A few thousand years later, people created beeswax or animal fat candles.

Solving a Puzzle

Throughout history people were curious about the nature of light. They knew that the sun's light provided light, warmth, and food. But how did light work? For thousands of years, different people came up with theories about the nature of light.

Pythagoras lived in ancient Greece in 500 BCE. He was one of the first people to propose ideas about how light worked. He thought that everything visible was emitting a stream of light particles. Sir Isaac Newton agreed with the particle theory. He studied light in the 1660s CE. In fact Newton was the first to record that sunlight contains all the colors of the EM spectrum.

Sir Isaac Newton studied colors and light.

Christian Huygens was another scientist during Newton's time. He had a different idea about how light travels. He found that light acts more like a wave. In time most other scientists thought that Huygens was right. In 1864 physicist James Clerk Maxwell announced that light was an EM wave.

Finally in 1905 scientist Albert Einstein figured out what was really going on when light traveled. Light is both waves and particles. He discovered that light acts like particles when atoms absorb it. An atom is the smallest part of anything on Earth. But when light travels, it spreads out and makes ripples like a wave.

Light Inventions

Many inventors were figuring out ways to create light. They wanted light that was safer and lasted longer than candles and oil lamps. In 1792 inventor William Murdock figured out how to produce gas by heating coal. The gas made light when burned. Gas lighting became a popular source of light in homes and businesses, as well as in streetlights.

Thomas Edison experimented with electric lighting starting in 1877. Others had experimented before, but Edison found a better way using a vacuum pump invented by chemist Herman Sprengel in 1865. The pump removed the air from inside the glass bulb. This stopped the filament inside the lightbulb from

Thomas Edison's lightbulb design is still used today.

burning up. An incandescent filament lamp makes light when electricity heats a thin strip of wire until it gets hot enough to glow. In 1880 Edison got a patent for the incandescent filament lamp.

A Better Lightbulb

Edison's invention is still in use today. We also have fluorescent and other kinds of lighting systems. Fluorescent lights make light in a different way. Mercury vapor is inside a glass tube that has a special coating. Electricity changes the vapor into ions. This makes the tube light up. Ions are electrically charged atoms.

In 1962 Nick Holonyak Jr. invented a red light-emitting diode (LED). In 1993 Professor Shuji Nakamura created the first white LED. An LED bulb emits light without getting very hot when an electric current flows through it. It uses much less energy to produce the same amount of light.

Lots of Light

Most people use incandescent lightbulbs similar to the ones invented in the 1800s. These bulbs tend to waste most of their energy creating heat. The more modern lighting systems, such as fluorescent and LED, use far less electricity and generally last longer. Over time they can save money on energy bills.

In a book by author George S. Bryan, Thomas Edison is quoted on the process of inventing the electric light. Bryan wrote:

> *"The electric light," said Edison in later years, "has caused me the greatest amount of study, and has required the most elaborate experiments, although I was never myself discouraged, or inclined to be hopeless of success. I cannot say the same for all my associates. And yet through all those years of experimenting and research I never once made a discovery. All my work was deductive, and the results I achieved were those of invention pure and simple. I would construct a theory and work on its lines until I found it untenable, then it would be discarded at once and another theory evolved. This way was the only possible way for me to work out the problem."*
>
> *Source: George S. Bryan. Edison, the Man and His Work. London, New York: A.A. Knopf, 1926. Print. 109.*

What's the Big Idea?

Take a close look at Edison's words. What is his main idea? What evidence is used to support his point? Come up with a few sentences showing how Edison uses two or three pieces of evidence to support his main point.

CHAPTER THREE

Seeing Light

Our eyes can detect visible light. It travels as waves and particles in straight lines. But what happens when light shines on an object? Some of the light is reflected off the object. Some of the light is absorbed into the object. The absorbed light becomes heat. The reflected light is what allows us to see the object. Some objects reflect more light than others. It depends on how smooth or rough the

Water in a lake reflects sunlight but also absorbs some as heat.

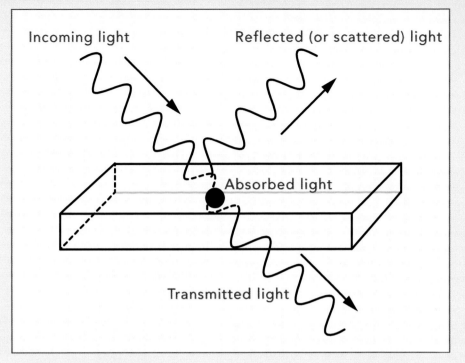

Light and Objects
This diagram shows how light reacts with an object. The incoming light might be reflected off the object. Some light is absorbed. And some of the light might transmit through the object. Compare this diagram with what is explained in the text. How is the information similar? How is the information different?

objects are. If it is a bumpy surface, light will scatter as it reflects.

Sometimes light passes right through an object, such as clear glass or clean water. It makes the object seem almost invisible to us. This is called transmission. Light waves might bend as they transmit.

A straw looks bent in a glass of water.

This bending is called refraction. Refraction happens because the light slows down as it passes through the object. Refraction can play tricks on our eyes. If you put a straw in a glass of water, is it bent? No, but refraction makes it looks as if it is.

If light comes from one direction, an object will cast a shadow. The shadow shows the outline of whatever is blocking the light.

Color the World

The EM spectrum is made up of waves that have different colors and different wavelengths. Red has the longest wavelength. Orange is next to red. Then yellow, green, blue, and violet follow. Each color has a shorter wavelength than the last. Red, blue, and green are the primary colors of the visible color spectrum. Combining two primary colors creates secondary colors.

When light hits an object, the waves that reflect from the object are the colors we see. Plants absorb all but the green

Rainbows

Sunlight and water combine to make a rainbow appear in the sky. The colors in sunlight separate in drops of water. Light reflects out of the drops at angles. Different drops reflect different colors. Many drops together form the stripes of a rainbow.

A rainbow reflects off the water in Ireland.

wavelength. That's why most plants look green to us in spring and summer.

Our eyes have three kinds of color sensors. The sensors are called cones. Each cone picks up a primary color—red, green, or blue.

Pigments are materials that absorb colors. Pigments are used in paint to make it reflect only certain color wavelengths. An object appears black when it absorbs all colors. Black is the color you see if there is no light at all reaching your eye. You see white when all colors reach your eye. White paint absorbs no colors.

What we see depends on light. What absorbs or reflects light gives us all the amazing forms and colors of our world. Without light the world would be colorless.

Astronomer and author Carl Sagan wrote about light and how we see colors in his book *Pale Blue Dot: A Vision of the Human Future in Space*. He wrote:

> *It is sometimes said that scientists are unromantic, that their passion to figure out robs the world of beauty and mystery. But is it not stirring to understand how the world actually works—that white light is made of colors, that color is the way we perceive the wavelengths of light, that transparent air reflects light, that in so doing it discriminates among the waves, and that the sky is blue for the same reason that the sunset is red? It does no harm to the romance of the sunset to know a little bit about it.*
>
> Source: Carl Sagan. Pale Blue Dot: A Vision of the Human Future in Space. New York: Ballantine, 1994. Print. 130–131.

Consider Your Audience

Read Sagan's speech closely. How could you adapt the speech for a different audience, such as your parents or younger friends? Write a blog post conveying this same information for the new audience. What is the best way to get your point across to this audience?

CHAPTER FOUR

Light on the Job

Light does a lot more than give us the ability to see the world. Light is used in many ways in our personal lives. Light helps the world survive and flourish. Some areas of the world can grow plants almost all year long because of the amount of sunlight they receive. People can use artificial light to grow plants in areas without as much sun or when it is not a good growing season. Scientists developed special

Rainforests receive a lot of light year-round and have very long growing seasons.

bulbs that provide the best light for growing plants.

Solar Energy

The sun's energy is an amazing resource. The earliest architects took advantage of the sun's natural light when they designed buildings. The best design made use of the sun's heat in winter and would block it in summer. Windows allowed light to come in. People could see without using artificial light. Shade from trees planted in the right places could block the sun in summer. In winter when the trees lost their leaves, the building could absorb heat from the sun's light. When used in this way, the sun's energy is called passive solar energy.

Solar panels collect light and turn it into energy that can be used in a home.

Solar energy can also be collected and moved to where it is needed. Solar panels collect the sun's energy. The panels are usually flat boxes that are painted black on the inside and have glass covers. They sit on rooftops or are mounted on stands. These solar panels collect the sun's energy in pipes filled with liquid. The heated liquid can be used to heat water, rooms, or power a cooling system. This is active solar energy.

Scientists found that when the sun hit certain materials, they would produce electricity. They used these materials to make solar cells. Solar cells power some traffic signs and satellites, as well as some homes.

Light and Optics

Optics is the study of light and images. The lenses in our eyes cause an image to form at the back of the eye. Cameras, microscopes, telescopes, and binoculars also use lenses. Lenses are usually made of glass or plastic and are clear. The lenses in microscopes, telescopes, and binoculars help us see objects more clearly even if they are very tiny or very far away.

Dark Moods

Some people get depressed during the shorter days of winter. The condition is called seasonal affective disorder (SAD). People with SAD become moody and less energetic. It's hard for them to concentrate, and they might sleep a lot. One treatment for SAD is light. Light therapy imitates a sunny day.

Special lenses in telescopes help us see things that are very far away.

The lenses in a pair of glasses or contact lenses help correct vision problems. Glasses for people who have trouble seeing things that are far away have lenses that are concave. Concave lenses are thinner in the middle than they are on the edges. They make light rays bend outward. Glasses for people who have trouble seeing things that are close up have lenses that are convex. Convex lenses are thicker in the

31

Fiber-optic cables send light signals.

middle than they are on the edges. They cause light rays to come together.

Fiber Optics and Laser Light

Fiber optics are thin strands of glass or plastic used to carry laser light. The light is trapped inside the strands. The light can travel for thousands of miles. Fiber-optic cables were invented in 1970. These cables stretch across the world. Light signals are sent through the cables. These signals carry an amazing amount of information.

Laser light shines in a single direction. A lens can focus laser light to a very small spot. Bar code readers use laser light, as do some printers, video and audio discs, and medical devices.

FURTHER EVIDENCE

There is quite a bit of information about how light is useful to people in Chapter Four. It covered different ways we use light today. But if you could pick out the main point of the chapter, what would it be? What evidence was given to support that point? Visit the Web site below to learn more about solar energy. Choose a quote from the Web site that relates to this chapter. Does this quote support the author's main point? Does it make a new point? Write a few sentences explaining how the quote you found relates to this chapter.

Energy Kids: Solar
www.eia.gov/kids/energy.cfm?page=solar_home-basics

CHAPTER FIVE

Light Fantastic

Nature creates its own light shows. We can watch the sky on almost any clear night and see a meteor shoot across the sky. Space is full of meteors. They are rocks that sometimes strike and enter Earth's atmosphere. When they do that, they leave a trail of light that we can see.

Comets also zip through the sky. Comets are huge chunks of icy rocks that float in space. They

The Hale-Bopp comet was seen over England in 2009.

Green aurora light swirls above Kvaloya Island at Tromso, Norway, in the Arctic Circle.

reflect light from the sun. As they get close to the sun, they heat up. Some of the ice melts and creates a tail of small debris that follows the comet. If Earth passes through the comet's path, the stream becomes a meteor shower.

Auroras

Auroras are beautiful light shows in the sky. They can appear in the northern or southern sky. The light flickers on the horizon. Then glowing masses of green, blue, and red light waves appear. They swirl in the night sky before slowly fading away.

Auroras are electrically charged particles that are blown by solar wind. They speed along Earth's upper atmosphere. There they collide with gas atoms. The atoms give off light. The best places to see auroras are close to Earth's poles. That is where magnetic field lines enter Earth.

Bright Bolts

Lightning is powerful and also dangerous. Astronomers have observed lightning on the planets Saturn, Venus, and Jupiter. Lightning is common, but much of it is a mystery. Somehow electric charges develop on certain clouds. Small drops of water and ice crystals carry the charges. An electrical circuit is formed when huge amounts of electrical current jump between the cloud and the ground. The circuit lights up as the energy is released.

All Aglow

The oceans at night can glow with colorful, glittering lights. Organisms in the water have bioluminescence. This is a light made through a chemical reaction in their bodies. It makes them glow in the dark.

Bioluminescence is an important source of light in the oceans, especially in the darkest depths. Most bioluminescent plants and animals live in the oceans. But there are plants and animals on land that can also glow. Fireflies can produce light. They flash their lights to say hello or to warn enemies that they taste bad.

The woods might be glowing too. In fall the dead leaves and wood sometimes emit a soft glow of light called

Flashy Arms

One type of deep-sea octopus doesn't have suckers on its arms. Instead it has rows of bright flashing lights. These are called photophores. Some creatures in the sea are attracted to light. This octopus uses its flashy arms to lure animals that it wants to eat. Then it grabs and traps the animals. It also spreads its arms and flashes its lights to scare off other animals.

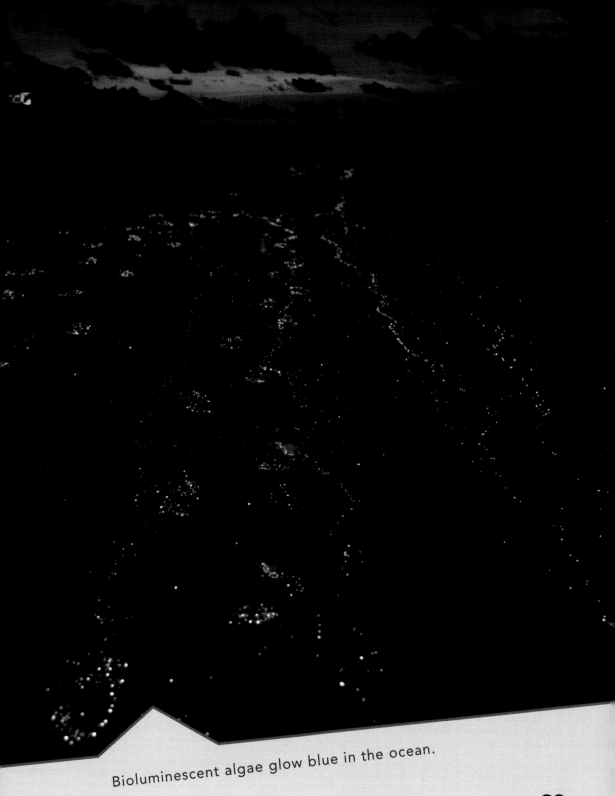

Bioluminescent algae glow blue in the ocean.

foxfire. This is a fungus that emits light as it eats rotting wood.

People have always depended on light to survive. We have learned to use light for electricity and different tools. Light lets us see things all the way to outer space. We have used the sun's energy to heat our homes and grow our food. Without light we would not be here. Our life on Earth depends on light every day.

EXPLORE ONLINE

The focus in Chapter Five was light found in nature. It also touched upon animals that make their own kind of light. The Web site below focuses on animals that produce light. As you know, every source is different. How is the information given in the Web site different from the information in this chapter? What information is the same? How do the two sources present information differently? What can you learn from this Web site?

Light Alive!: Bioluminescence
www.sdnhm.org/archive/kids/lightsalive/biolum2.html

Lights glow in a city at night.

IMPORTANT DATES

more than 400,000 years ago
People begin using fire.

500 BCE
Pythagoras proposes ideas about how light works.

1660s CE
Sir Isaac Newton records that sunlight contains all the colors of the EM spectrum.

1670s
Ole Roemer calculates the speed of light.

1792
William Murdock figures out how to produce gas from coal, which produces light when burned.

1864
James Clerk Maxwell announces that light is really an EM wave.

1880
Thomas Alva Edison gets a patent for the incandescent filament lamp.

1905
Albert Einstein explains that light is both particles and waves.

1962
Nick Holonyak Jr. invents a red light-emitting diode (LED).

1970
Fiber-optic cables are invented.

1993
Professor Shuji Nakamura creates the first white LED.

OTHER WAYS YOU CAN FIND LIGHT IN THE REAL WORLD

Photography and Light

Light is used to create photographs. If light passes through a small hole, it will reflect an image on the opposing surface. Photography uses film that is sensitive to light. Or a digital sensor in a digital camera records the image created by light.

Prisms

Do you want to see all the colors in light? You can make your own rainbow by using a prism. A prism is a see-through object that is cut with precise angles and flat planes. You hang a prism in a window where sunlight shines through. The sunlight hits one side of the prism and exits on the other sides. The light refracts and separates into the colors of the rainbow.

Studying Cancer

In 2009 doctors figured out a way to use light to study how and why cancer spreads. They can control the protein in a living cell and study how it functions. The light is shined on the cell. This causes the protein to react. Researchers can learn more about cancer cells and how they grow and behave. This new tool for studying cells will hopefully help researchers find treatments and cures for cancer.

Dig Deeper

What questions do you still have about the EM spectrum? Do you want to learn more about how light travels? Or how to save energy when using light? Write down one or two questions that can guide you in doing research. With an adult's help, find a few reliable new sources about light that can help answer your questions. Write a few sentences about how you did your research and what you learned from it.

Another View

There are many sources online and in your library about light. Ask a librarian or other adult to help you find a reliable source on light. Compare what you learn in this new source and what you have found out in this book. Then write a short essay comparing and contrasting the new source's view of light to the ideas in this book. How are they different? How are they similar? Why do you think they are different or similar?

Why Do I Care?

This book explains how light is used every day. List two or three ways that you use light in your life. For example, imagine a day without light. What would be difficult about that day?

Take a Stand

This book focuses on light in our world. It also gives some information about new discoveries about light. Which of these discoveries do you think had a more lasting impact on society? Why? Write a short essay explaining your opinion. Include your reasons for your opinion, and give some facts and details to support those reasons.

GLOSSARY

atmosphere
the mixture of gases that
surrounds a planet

atom
the tiniest part of an element
that has all the properties of
that element

bioluminescence
light made in a chemical
reaction within animals

chlorophyll
the green substance in
plants that uses light to
make food from carbon
dioxide and water

electromagnetic
referring to the connection
between electric and
magnetic waves

EM spectrum
the range of colors that is
revealed when light shines
through a prism or drops
of water

fluorescent
giving out a bright light by
using a certain type of energy

incandescent
glowing with intense light
and heat

photosynthesis
a chemical process by which
green plants make their food

refract
when a light ray changes
direction by passing from one
medium to another, such as
air to water

transmit
to pass through something

LEARN MORE

Books

Goldsmith, Michael. *Light and Sound*. Boston: Kingfisher, 2007.

Halpern, Monica. *All About Lights*. Washington, DC: National Geographic, 2006.

Riley, Peter D. *Light*. Mankato, MN: Sea-to-Sea Publications, 2011.

Web Links

To learn more about light, visit ABDO Publishing Company online at **www.abdopublishing.com**. Web sites about light are featured on our Book Links page. These links are routinely monitored and updated to provide the most current information available. Visit **www.mycorelibrary.com** for free additional tools for teachers and students.

INDEX

ABOUT THE AUTHOR

Robin Koontz is author and illustrator of many books and articles for children and young adults. Her 2011 science book was an Animal Behavior Society Outstanding Children's Book Award Finalist. Koontz lives with her husband in the Coast Range of western Oregon.